weblinks

You don't need a computer to use this book. But, for readers who do have access to the Internet, the book provides links to recommended websites which offer additional information and resources on the subject.

You will find weblinks boxes like this on some pages of the book.

---
weblinks

For more information about Kylie Minogue, go to www.waylinks.co.uk /21CentLives/PopStars
---

waylinks.co.uk

To help you find the recommended websites easily and quickly, weblinks are provided on our own website, **waylinks.co.uk.** These take you straight to the relevant websites and save you typing in the Internet address yourself.

Internet safety

↗ Never give out personal details, which include: your name, address, school, telephone number, email address, password and mobile number.

↗ Do not respond to messages which make you feel uncomfortable – tell an adult.

↗ Do not arrange to meet in person someone you have met on the Internet.

↗ Never send your picture or anything else to an online friend without a parent's or teacher's permission.

↗ If you see anything that worries you, tell an adult.

A note to adults
Internet use by children should be supervised. We recommend that you install filtering software which blocks unsuitable material.

Website content

The weblinks for this book are checked and updated regularly. However, because of the nature of the Internet, the content of a website may change at any time, or a website may close down without notice. While the Publishers regret any inconvenience this may cause readers, they cannot be responsible for the content of any website other than their own.

WAYLAND

21st CENTURY LIVES
POP STARS

Kay Woodward

WAYLAND

© Copyright 2006 Wayland

Editors: Kirsty Hamilton / Sarah Gay
Design: Peter Bailey for Proof Books
Cover design: Hodder Children's Books

Published in Great Britain in 2006 by Wayland,
an imprint of Hachette Children's Books.

Reprinted in 2006

The right of Kay Woodward to be identified as the author of the work has been
asserted by her in accordance with the Copyright, Designs and Patents Act 1988.

British Library Cataloguing in Publication Data
Woodward, Kay
Pop stars. - (21st century lives)
1. Rock musicians - biography - Juvenile literature
I. Title
782.42166'0922

ISBN-10: 0750248092
ISBN-13: 9780750248099

Cover: Robbie Williams performs on stage at the 10th Annual 'Rock the Vote' Awards
in 2003.

Picture acknowledgements: 4, 5, 7, 8, Title page and 10, 11, 19, 20, 21 Reuters/Corbis;
6 Gregory Pace/Corbis; 9 Duomo/Corbis; 12 Darren Staples/Reuters/Corbis; 13 Toby
Melville/Reuters/Corbis; 14 Stephane Cardinale/People Avenue/Corbis; 15 Rune
Hellestad/Corbis; Cover and 16 Steve Azzara/Corbis; 17 Rune Hellestad/Corbis; 18
Steve Sands/New York Newswire/Corbis

Printed in China by WKT Company Ltd

Wayland
an imprint of Hachette Children's Books
338 Euston Road
London NW1 3BH

Contents

Britney Spears
Schoolgirl Star

Britney Spears has been an international star since the age of seventeen.

❝One of the true joys of my life and career has been trying out new things. I've loved every step of this journey I'm on. I love singing and dancing and acting and songwriting... it all energizes and inspires me. ❞

Britney Spears offical website (britneyspears.com)

Name: Britney Jean Spears

Date and place of birth: 2 December 1981, Kentwood, Louisiana, USA

Background: Britney began dance lessons when she was just five years old, and gymnastics two years later. She appeared in the Disney Channel's *New Mickey Mouse Club* from the age of eleven. In 1997, she signed with Jive Records.

First hit: *...Baby One More Time* (1999)

Albums: *...Baby One More Time* (1999), *Oops! ...I Did It Again* (2000), *Britney* (2001), *In the Zone* (2003), *Greatest Hits: My Prerogative* (2004)

Career highs: In 1999, Britney became the youngest artist to top the US Billboard Hot 100 Chart *and* the youngest artist to achieve a number one album at the same time. She received a star on the Hollywood Walk of Fame in 2003. In 2005, she won her first Grammy award for Best Dance Recording for *Toxic*. She formed the Britney Spears Foundation, which helps children in need.

Sponsorship: Pepsi. *Curious*, her Elizabeth Arden fragrance, is a top seller.

Something you might not know about her: In 2000, Britney Spears starred in an episode of *The Simpsons* – as herself.

Marital status: Britney married backing dancer Kevin Federline in 2004.

At the age of nine, Britney Spears moved to New York City with her mother and younger sister. She went in search of fame and, after studying for three years at the Professional Performing Arts School, she found it on the Disney Channel's *New Mickey Mouse Club*. Next, she auditioned for pop groups, soon winning a recording deal. Britney was on her way!

When she was seventeen, Britney Spears stormed the charts with the hit single *...Baby One More Time*. She became famous around the world. But many wondered if it was just her youth, zest and energy that appealed to fans. Would Britney continue to be as popular as she grew older?

Britney's first album sold a phenomenal twenty-five million copies worldwide and her total album sales add up to over seventy-five million copies! Her long list of hit singles includes *Oops!... I Did It Again, Everytime* and *Toxic*, all of which reached number one in the UK charts. Her amazing dance performances, both live and on video, have contributed towards her success.

She has grown up in the spotlight of the world's media. But Britney's ever-changing image has helped her to make the transition from teen sensation to fully-fledged pop star. She has performed in a school uniform, a red rubber catsuit and even a wedding dress. Her look is always inventive and never dull.

In 2002, Britney took a break from the pop world to star in her first film. *Crossroads* is about friendship and discovery – the story of three best friends who take a trip across the USA. Not surprisingly, Britney plays a girl who is destined to make it big as a singer. The film is a real treat for her fans!

Britney's personal life is often splashed across newpapers and celebrity magazines. She and her first serious boyfriend, popstar Justin Timberlake, were often photographed together. They became engaged, but shocked their fans by splitting in 2002. Britney and Justin blamed their busy work schedules for the split and are said to remain on good terms.

Both Britney's live performances and her outfits are dazzling.

In January 2004, Britney married one of her oldest friends, Jason Allen Alexander, in Las Vegas. The marriage lasted just 55 hours. But later that year, she tied the knot again. This time she married Kevin Federline, one of her former backing dancers. The ceremony was top secret and attended only by family and close friends.

"I want to do nothing but support her and praise her and wish her the best."

Madonna
All Pop Music
(AllPop.com)

weblinks

For more information about Britney Spears, go to
www.waylinks.co.uk/21CentLives/PopStars

Beyoncé is famous as a member of Destiny's Child and as a solo artist.

> **"**...this record [*Dangerously in Love*] was a chance for me to grow as a writer and a singer... I felt free because I could go into the studio and talk about whatever I wanted, but in many ways it was actually harder to be on my own creatively. I depend so much on Destiny's Child to tell me if they like something or not. I'm so critical of myself that it's scary to have to depend on your own instincts. **"**

Thread (www.thread.co.nz)

Name: Beyoncé Giselle Knowles

Date and place of birth: 4 September 1981, Houston, Texas, USA

Background: Beyoncé went to the High School for Performing and Visual Arts in her hometown of Houston.

First hit: With Destiny's Child – *No, no, no* (1997); Solo – *Crazy in Love* (2003)

Albums: With Destiny's Child – *Destiny's Child* (1998), *The Writing's on the Wall* (1999), *Survivor* (2001), *8 Days of Christmas* (2001), *This Is The Remix* (2002), *Destiny Fulfilled* (2004); Solo – *Dangerously In Love* (2003)

Career highs: Winning the 2001 ASCAP Pop Songwriter of the Year Award. Winning five awards at the 2004 Grammy Awards.

Sponsorship: Pepsi, L'Oreal and Tommy Hilfiger.

Something you might not know about her: The Destiny's Child voice coach and stylist is Beyoncé's mum, and the band's manager is Beyoncé's dad!

Marital status: Beyoncé's boyfriend is top US rapper Jay-Z.

As Destiny's Child, Michelle Williams (left), Beyoncé Knowles (centre) and Kelly Rowland (right), set the stage alight with their singing and dancing.

Beyoncé Knowles was just nine years old when she met LaTavia Roberson and the pair started to sing and rap together. They called themselves GirlTyme, but later gained two band members and a new name – Destiny's Child. Their first recording featured on the *Men in Black* soundtrack, but it was *No, no, no*, a single from their debut album, that really got the group noticed in the US and the UK.

After a change in the band's line-up, Destiny's Child followed up their success with another two hit albums – *The Writing's On The Wall* (1999) and *Survivor* (2001) – before stunning their fans with some unexpected news. Beyoncé, Kelly Rowland and Michelle Williams had decided to take time off from Destiny's Child so that they could each work on their own material.

Beyoncé threw herself into a number of different projects. She and rapper Jay-Z featured on each other's tracks, and they later started dating each other. Next, Beyoncé recorded a duet with legendary R&B artist Luther Vandross. Then, in 2003, she released her first solo album – *Dangerously In Love*. It topped the charts on both sides of the Atlantic.

As the main songwriter in Destiny's Child, Beyoncé co-wrote many hit songs, including *Say My Name*, which won two Grammys in 2001. The same year, her success was recognised by the American Society of Composers, Authors and Publishers, who gave her the Songwriter of the Year Award. Beyoncé was only the second woman ever to win the Award and the first African American woman to do so. Unbelievably, Beyoncé eclipsed this success in 2004 by winning five Grammy Awards in the USA and the Best International Female Artist Brit Award in the UK.

Beyoncé is one of the few pop stars to have successfully made it in the movie business. In 2002, she co-starred with Mike Myers in the third Austin Powers film. Her next big roles were in *The Fighting Temptations* (2003) and alongside Steve Martin in *The Pink Panther* (2005).

"Beyoncé Knowles's *Crazy in Love* was the year's moment of absolute perfection, a single heard everywhere from R&B clubs to Top of the Pops to the decidedly non bling-bling environs of Glastonbury."

The Guardian, December 2003

weblinks

For more information about Beyoncé, go to
www.waylinks.co.uk/21CentLives/PopStars

Jennifer Lopez
Jenny from the Block

Jennifer Lopez made the successful leap from movies to music.

"I am still the same girl who grew up in the Bronx, with my head full of limitless dreams. I still wake up thinking about everything that I want to achieve."

Jennifer Lopez – an unauthorised biography **by Patricia J Duncan**

Name: Jennifer Lynn López

Date and place of birth: 24 July 1970, Castle Hill, the Bronx, New York City, USA

Background: Jennifer danced from the age of five, becoming a professional dancer as soon as she left school. After getting into acting, she starred in films with George Clooney and Wesley Snipes. In 1999, she launched her singing career.

First hit: *If You Had My Love* (1999)

Albums: *On The 6* (1999), *J.Lo* (2001), *J To Tha L-O! The Remixes* (2002), *This Is Me… Then* (2002), *Rebirth* (2005)

Career highs: In 2001, Jennifer became the first woman to have a number one film and a number one album in the USA at the same time. Her first single reached number one in more than forty different countries.

Sponsorship: Pepsi. She owns her own clothing line called *J. Lo by Jennifer Lopez* and two fragrances – *Glow* and *Still.*

Something you might not know about her: Jennifer was sacked from a New York City clothes store when she was fifteen. The reason? She danced too much!

Marital status: Jennifer married singer-songwriter Marc Anthony in 2004.

Dancing was Jennifer's ticket to fame and fortune. When she was young she went to dance classes nearly every day, learning ballet, jazz and flamenco. At the weekend she travelled into Manhattan for extra ballet lessons. After leaving school she toured Europe, before becoming a backing dancer for Janet Jackson. This led to acting parts on television and in film. But the title role in *Selena* (1997) – the story of a famous Mexican-American pop star – reminded her how much she liked dancing. It also showed her what an exhilarating experience singing in front of an audience could be.

Of all celebrities to suffer at the hands of the paparazzi, Jennifer Lopez has received perhaps the most excessive media attention. After her high-profile relationship with rap artist P. Diddy, she had become one of the world's most photographed women. Then she became engaged to film star Ben Affleck and the press went wild. By September 2003, the pressure was so unbearable that Jennifer and Ben split – the day before their wedding day. Since then, Jennifer has done her best to keep her private life just that – private.

Jennifer's music is a mixture of hip-hop, Latin and pop. To keep her tracks sounding fresh and original she likes to work with different music producers. And Jennifer has worked with the best, including Emilio Estefan, Rodney Jerkins and P. Diddy.

Jennifer has invited many famous hip-hop and R&B stars to feature on her tracks. LL Cool J, Fat Joe, Ja Rule and Big Punisher have all sung with her. One of the duettists she worked with was Marc Anthony – famous for music described as tropical and pop. Jennifer got on with him so well that she married him in June 2004!

Jennifer has performed at great sporting events, including the 1999 FIFA Women's World Cup.

Jennifer Lopez is one of the few artists with chart-topping careers in both music and film. She hit the big screen in 1995, then went on to release her first single, *If You Had My Love*, four years later. So what was her recipe for success? Talent and luck? Asbolutely. But there is no doubt that hard work, dedication and pure ambition have also helped Jennifer to become the star she is today.

"She works very hard and I respect her for that."
Ja Rule on the Channel 5 documentary about J. Lo's life.

weblinks

For more information about Jennifer Lopez, go to
www.waylinks.co.uk/21CentLives/PopStars

Kylie Minogue
The Princess of Pop

When Kylie and Justin Timberlake duetted at the 2003 Brit Awards, their song was the highlight of the show.

> **The point of my job is to entertain and make it look easy, so I guess it's the parts you don't often see which make me feel proud. All the behind-the-scenes work, the fears and insecurities I have to face and overcome to improve myself as a person and performer, all of the people who believe in me and encourage me.**

Kylie Minogue official website (kylie.com)

Name: Kylie Ann Minogue

Date and place of birth: 28 May 1968, Melbourne, Australia

Background: Kylie first appeared on TV when she was just eleven years old, starring in an Australian soap opera. She left school when she was seventeen to become a full-time actress. Two years later, she released her first single.

First hit: *Locomotion* (1987)

Albums: *Kylie* (1988), *Enjoy Yourself* (1989), *Rhythm of Love* (1990). *Let's Get To It* (1991). *Kylie Minogue* (1994), *Impossible Princess* (1998), *Light Years* (2000), *Fever* (2001), *Body Language* (2003). Kylie has also released many other remix and compilation albums.

Career highs: Her first thirteen singles all reached the UK top ten. She performed at the 2000 Sydney Olympic Games. Kylie has reached number one during each of the last three decades – the only other female performer to achieve this feat is Madonna.

Sponsorship: She owns her own range of underwear, called *Love Kylie*.

Something you might not know about her: Her favourite cartoon character is Mr Burns from *The Simpsons*.

Marital status: Kylie's boyfriend is French actor Olivier Martinez.

Kylie Minogue is so famous that she is recognised by her first name alone. But she wasn't always a pop star – she spent her teenage years acting in Australian dramas and soap operas. It was during a singing performance in Melbourne that she realised her future could lie in music rather than TV. After quitting Australian soap opera *Neighbours* in 1987, she released her first single – *Locomotion*. It was a huge hit, especially in her own country, and gave Kylie the confidence to start her international pop career.

The next ten years brought Kylie mixed pop success, but in 2000, her career was given a huge boost with the release of another single – *Spinning Around*. Both the track and the video put Kylie back in the spotlight and she shot straight to number one in the UK charts. Since then, she has racked up many more hits, including the staggeringly successful *Can't Get You Out of My Head* (2001), which reached number one in over 40 countries.

In 2002, Kylie won Brit Awards for Best International Female Solo Artist and Best International Album. The following year, her duet with Justin Timberlake was the highlight of the entire awards ceremony.

Despite an incredibly busy schedule, Kylie still finds time to act. She appears briefly in the smash-hit movie *Moulin Rouge!* (2001), which stars Nicole Kidman and Ewan McGregor. Kylie plays the part of the Green Fairy.

Kylie's live tours are legendary, with fantastic costumes and ever-changing sets. But perhaps her most memorable performance took place during the closing ceremony of the Sydney 2000 Olympic Games, where Kylie sang to an incredible four billion viewers around the world.

Kylie has been in the music business since the 1980s, when she was a teenager. So it's no surprise that her image has changed dramatically since she first started out. Her fun, schoolgirl appearance has metamorphosed into a sophisticated, older look – she won a Lifetime Achievement Award at the 2005 Elle Style Awards. Her reputation has changed too. At first, many critics refused to take Kylie's music seriously, but she is now regarded as one of pop music's greatest artists. She has sold over forty million singles and twenty-five million albums worldwide.

Kylie is famous for her vibrant live performances.

"No matter how brilliant or awful her musical output has been, her fame has remained a constant. She's beyond a surname, beyond mere records."

New Musical Express

weblinks

For more information about Kylie Minogue go to
www.waylinks.co.uk/21CentLives/PopStars

Lemar

A Pop Star Second-time Around

Lemar shot to fame on a TV talent show.

Name: Lemar Obika

Date and place of birth: 4 April 1978, London

Background: Lemar and his brothers used to pretend to be the Jackson Five – the pop group that Michael Jackson once belonged to. They performed in front of their parents. After leaving school, Lemar chose to follow a pop career rather than study pharmacy at university.

First hit: *Dance (With U)* (2004)

Albums: *Dedicated* (2003), *Time to Grow* (2004)

Career highs: Taking part in the BBC's Fame Academy. Performing with singing legend Lionel Richie. Winning the award for Best Urban Act in the 2004 Brit Awards.

Musical influences: He thinks R Kelly is an amazing songwriter and admires soul king Marvin Gaye for his unique singing ability.

Something you might not know about him: Lemar made his movie debut in *De-Lovely* – a film about famous songwriter Cole Porter. He sang to the film's stars, Kevin Kline and Ashley Judd – in a gondola!

Marital status: Lemar and his girlfriend Charmaine have been seeing each other for many years.

> **I try not to fit any song into any genre. I just take what I feel inside. Depending on which producer or writer I'm working with, I let the music speak for itself and hopefully it'll be soulful and mean something to me and the people around me.**
>
> **BBC Music**

Lemar performed in his first concert when he was just eighteen years old, supporting the legendary Usher in Tottenham, London. Over the next few years, he built his R&B reputation, even touring with Destiny's Child. At the age of twenty-five, he signed a terrific deal with a major record label and he had a brilliant future as a pop star ahead of him. Then things went wrong – Lemar's contract was cancelled because of changes within the record company.

Without an income, Lemar was forced to return to his desk job in a bank. It looked as if his dream of being a pop star was over… But not for long. When Lemar spotted an advert for the BBC's *Fame Academy*, he decided to give his pop career one last try. He entered the competition and reached the final round!

Fame Academy was Lemar's big break. For ten weeks he took lessons in how to be a popstar, undergoing a public vote each week. He impressed judges and TV viewers alike with his unmistakeable talent and his easy-going personality. For Lemar, the highlight of the entire show was performing the classic hit *Easy Like Sunday Morning* with Lionel Richie. Many were certain that Lemar would win and it was a huge shock when he came third. But nothing could stop him from being a star now.

As soon as *Fame Academy* was over, Lemar was invited to duet onstage with R&B star Beverly Knight. Then it was back to the studio to record his debut album – *Dedicated* – which went on to sell over half a million copies. Three singles were released from the album and all reached the UK top ten. Another hit album and singles followed.

One of the reasons Lemar is so successful may be because he is so versatile. He is as comfortable performing classic soul tracks as he is with modern R&B – he's commercial *and* cool. During his sell-out UK tours in 2004 and 2005, the audiences ranged from teen fans right through to Lemar's older admirers. One of his proudest moments was receiving an award for Best Urban Act at the 2004 Brit Awards. Lemar was no longer in third place – he'd won!

Lemar and Jamelia performed their own version of the classic track Addicted to Love *at the 2005 Brit Awards*

"There is no one in the academy who can interpret a song like Lemar interprets [The Al Green hit] *Let's Stay Together*."

Carrie Grant – vocal coach from *Fame Academy*.

weblinks

For more information about Lemar, go to
www.waylinks.co.uk/21CentLives/PopStars

Jamelia is a pop star, model and style icon.

Name: Jamelia Davis

Date and place of birth: 2 January 1981, Birmingham

Background: Jamelia signed to Parlophone when she was just fifteen years old. Her first single hit the charts when she was eighteen.

First hit: *I Do* (1999)

Albums: *Drama* (2000), *Thank You* (2003)

Career highs: Jamelia was nominated for five Mobo Awards in 2000 and won one. She was nominated for two Brit Awards in 2004 and three Brits in 2005, where she performed a memorable duet with Lemar at the awards ceremony. At the 2005 Capital FM Awards, she was voted Favourite UK Female Vocalist.

Sponsorship: Reebok, Pretty Polly.

Something you might not know about her: Jamelia has supported both Justin Timberlake and Misteeq on tour.

Marital status: Jamelia's boyfriend is footballer Darren Byfield.

"I'm not the British Beyoncé... I don't feel in competition with anyone. If anyone came on the scene similar to me I wouldn't feel threatened in any way, because I'm already here. "

Daily Mail

When Jamelia was growing up in the Midlands, she became a huge fan of urban R&B. Soon she was writing her own songs and, at the age of just fifteen, she got the chance to show the music business what she could do. At her record company audition, she stunned everyone at Parlophone by performing her own songs without backing tracks. They signed her up immediately, aware that they had a huge talent on their hands. But Parlophone also knew that Jamelia was very young and rather than push her into releasing material straight away, they decided to let her develop at her own pace – giving her time to finish school.

It was a good decision. Three years later, eighteen-year-old Jamelia released her first single, taken from her debut album, *Drama*. It was a hit and she became a pop star. Three more hits followed and Jamelia's music career was going from strength to strength when she broke the news that she was expecting a baby. Then, when Teja was born in 2001, Jamelia decided to take time off to look after her daughter. Many wondered how her music career could survive. Would Jamelia's fans remember her when she returned to the music scene? They did!

Jamelia returned to the world of pop in 2003 with *Bout*. But it was her next single, *Superstar*, that propelled her to the top of the UK charts. It was also a massive international hit, doing well in Europe, Australia and New Zealand.

Jamelia writes most of her own material and loves to experiment with new sounds and styles. Working with different artists is another way of making sure that her music always sounds fresh. She worked with Bubba Sparxxx on *Club Hoppin'* and Asher D of So Solid Crew on *Off Da Enz*. One of her most popular collaborations featured a guest vocal from Beenie Man, *Money*, which in 2000, reached number 5 in the UK charts. Chris Martin from Coldplay wrote the track *See It In A Boy's Eyes* for her.

So what's in store for Jamelia? She signed a deal with Naomi Campbell's modelling agency in 2004 and would like to make a move to the big screen in the future. But for now, she is happy to remain true to her R&B roots.

In 2005, Jamelia performed at the 'Make Poverty History' rally in Trafalgar Square, London.

"A poised nineteen year old, Jamelia has the home-grown talent to give Missy Elliot a run for her money."

Independent on Sunday

weblinks

For more information about Jamelia, go to
www.waylinks.co.uk/21CentLives/PopStars

Robbie Williams
The Ultimate Entertainer

Robbie Williams' live performances are legendary.

❝I want you to remember something for me. My name is Robbie Williams. I'm a singer, a songwriter and a born entertainer. ❞

Live at Knebworth Park, Summer 2003

Name: Robert Peter Williams

Date and place of birth: 13 February 1974, Stoke-on-Trent, Staffordshire

Background: Robbie became a member of the phenomenally successful boy band Take That in 1991. The band split in 1996, but by this time, Robbie had already left to pursue a solo career in pop.

First hit: With Take That – *Do What You Like* (1991); Solo – *Freedom* (1996)

Albums: With Take That – *Take That and Party* (1992), *Everything Changes* (1993), *Nobody Else* (1995), *Greatest Hits* (1996); Solo – *Life Thru a Lens* (1997), *I've Been Expecting You* (1998), *The Ego Has Landed* (1999), *Sing When You're Winning* (2000), *Swing When You're Winning* (2001), *Escapology* (2002), *Robbie Williams – Live At Knebworth* (2003), *Greatest Hits* (2004), *Intensive Care* (2005)

Career highs: Being voted one of the 100 Greatest Britons in the BBC's nationwide poll in 2002. Performing three gigs in front of more than a million fans in Knebworth Park in 2003. Winning the award for the best song from the previous twenty-five years at the 2005 Brit Awards. Robbie has won a record fifteen Brit Awards in total.

In his spare time: Robbie set up the charity Give It Sum, which is based in his home town. He is also a huge supporter of the Comic Relief charity.

Something you might not know about him: Robbie Williams used to work as a florist and as a double-glazing salesman.

Marital status: Robbie Williams is single, but was once engaged to singer Nicole Appleton.

Whenever Robbie Williams appears on stage, audiences go wild!

Hit single followed hit single. *Let Me Entertain You* reached number three in the UK charts, then in 1998 *Millennium* reached the coveted number one spot. His albums have been equally successful, most reaching number one in the UK charts.

In 2001, after more number one hits with *She's the One* and *Rock DJ*, Robbie's career veered off in an entirely new direction. He moved from 21st century pop back to a style of singing that was popular in the 1950s – swing. And even though his new album, *Swing When You're Winning*, was utterly unlike anything he'd done before, it too was a hit. The laid-back *Somethin' Stupid*, a duet with Oscar-winning actress Nicole Kidman which was taken from the album, reached number one.

Robbie's personal life often makes the headlines. His battle against alcohol and drug addiction has been highly publicised, while his relationships with Geri Halliwell and Rachel Hunter made headlines around the world. He now lives quietly in Los Angeles, USA, where he has a more healthy and private lifestyle. Robbie Williams' tracks are well known for their inventive lyrics and memorable tunes. Fans have Robbie himself and his brilliant songwriting partners – Guy Chambers, followed by Stephen Duffy – to thank for the music, which has won Robbie three Brit Awards for Best Single.

Even when he was young, Robbie Williams loved to entertain people. At school he was known as the class joker and, out of school, he appeared in musicals and plays performed by the local theatre group. Then his mum spotted an advert for a boy band and Robbie became one of the most flamboyant members of Take That. Now he could entertain people as a pop star!

After leaving the band to become a solo performer, Robbie Williams' first single was *Freedom*. But it was his fifth release, *Angels*, that showed he had the potential to be even more successful than Take That. Although *Angels* only reached number four in the UK charts, it became a classic and, at the 2005 Brit Awards, was voted the best song for the years 1981–2005. It was this track that made Robbie famous throughout Europe.

Whether on stage or on video, Robbie's performances are guaranteed to be spellbinding. The ultimate showman, he likes to surprise and shock his audience, but most of all he just loves to entertain.

"As Robbie Williams descended the stage hanging by a wire, dressed in a black shirt and white tie, the hundreds and thousands of fans went wild…"

BBC Music

weblinks

For more information about Robbie Williams, go to
www.waylinks.co.uk/21CentLives/PopStars

Justin Timberlake
In Sync with Fame

The ultimate pin-up, Justin has fans all around the world.

Name: Justin Randall Timberlake

Date and place of birth: 31 January 1981, Memphis, Tennessee, USA

Background: Justin has been a singer ever since he was very young. He sang with a church choir when he was eight, won the Pre-teen Mr America Pageant when he was ten and appeared in a TV talent show when he was just eleven.

First hit: With *NSYNC – *I Want You Back* (1997); Solo – *Like I Love You* (2002)

Albums: With *NSYNC – *NSYNC (1998), *Home For Christmas* (1998), *Winter Album* (1998), *No Strings Attached* (2000), *Celebrity* (2001); Solo – *Justified* (2002)

Career highs: At the 2004 Brit Awards, he won the award for Best International Male Solo Artist. *Justified* was the Best International Album. In the US, he won two Grammy Awards for *Cry Me A River* and *Justified*.

Sponsorship: He set up the Justin Timberlake Foundation to help schools fund music and arts programmes.

Something you might not know about him: Justin's mum came up with the name *NSYNC. She took the last letter of each of the founder member's names – Justi**n**, Chri**s**, Joe**y**, Jaso**n** and J**C** – and simply put them together.

Marital status: Justin has been seeing US actress Cameron Diaz since 2003.

> **"There's still a chance that *NSYNC could get back together... Our relationship goes way deeper than records. We're friends – those are my brothers."**
>
> **Warner Bros Extra
> (extratv.warnerbros.com)**

He was once more famous for his relationship with Britney Spears than for his singing ability, but now Justin Timberlake is a pop star in his own right. As a member of top US boy band *NSYNC, he has also enjoyed massive solo success.

Justin always knew that he wanted to be a singer so at the age of twelve, he and his mother moved to Orlando, Florida. There, Justin auditioned for the Disney Channel's *New Mickey Mouse Club*. He was chosen from five thousand hopefuls! Justin appeared on the show for a year, singing and dancing with his fellow Mouseketeers – Britney Spears, Christina Aguilera and JC Chasez.

In 1995, Justin was asked to join a boy band and he jumped at the chance to become lead vocalist. The band was named *NSYNC and toured Europe, impressing audiences with their cool music and slick dance routines. Then they took the USA by storm, their first album selling over ten million copies. Further albums and tours boosted *NSYNC's popularity. Justin also got the chance to write new songs for the band – some became huge hits.

In 2001, after their incredibly successful *Celebrity* tour, the band members decided that it was time to take a break from *NSYNC. Justin took the opportunity to work on solo material – the result was his ground-breaking album, *Justified*.

Fans loved Justin's new material. The four singles released from his debut album – *Like I Love You, Cry Me A River, Rock Your Body* and *Señorita* – were all huge hits on both sides of the Atlantic. He won two Brit Awards in 2004 and two prestigious Grammy Awards in the US.

Justin Timberlake has mesmerised audiences at countless awards ceremonies.

Justin's relationships always attract masses of attention from the world's media. He and Britney Spears made a very popular couple. Later, when he became engaged to Hollywood actress Cameron Diaz, reporters were eager for details. But this is one area of Justin's life that he likes to keep very private.

What does the future hold for Justin Timberlake? He and the rest of *NSYNC may release more material. He may also work on his solo career. But one thing's for sure – whatever Justin does, he'll make the headlines.

weblinks

For more information about Justin Timberlake, go to
www.waylinks.co.uk/21CentLives/PopStars

"You have to admire the guts of the boy-band member who strikes out alone. There is a high risk of failure… However, Justin Timberlake has succeeded."

The Guardian

Usher
The Rapper Who Sings

Usher has been rapping his way to the top of the charts since 1994.

❝I've been building my career since I was a little boy because singing had always been what I wanted to do. At first I thought about playing [American] football, then I wanted to play basketball, but in the end it was all about the music. It's my biggest passion and my biggest joy. ❞

The official Usher website (usherworld.com)

Name: Usher Jamie Raymond IV

Date and place of birth: 14 October 1978, Chattanooga, Tennessee, USA

Background: Usher first sang in public at his local church, where his mother was the choir director. At the age of thirteen, he performed in a talent competition and was spotted by a representative from the LaFace record label. He released his first single a year later.

First hit: *Call Me A Mack* (1993)

Albums: *Usher* (1994), *My Way* (1997), *Live* (1999), *8701* (2001), *Confessions* (2004)

Career highs: In May 2004, Usher had three US top ten singles in the same week. That year, he became the first artist to spend more than six months with at least one single in the Billboard Hot 100 Singles Chart.

Additional career highlight: Usher has sold over 30 million albums worldwide.

Something you might not know about him: In his spare time, Usher tries to help young people. In the US, he has taken part in safety campaigns and also stressed the importance of staying on at school.

Marital status: Usher's girlfriend is model Eisha Brightwell.

Being one of the world's most successful R&B popstars would be enough for some people, but Usher is a songwriter, a producer and an actor too. Since he started out in 1993 he has racked up a phenomenal number of hit songs, building an impressive movie career at the same time. However, his first love remains music.

Usher was less than sixteen years old when he began recording his first album, but he was lucky enough to be given a very famous helping hand – it was co-produced by the legendary Sean 'P. Diddy' Combs. The album, and the three singles taken from it, gave Usher a good start in the music business. But rather than releasing a follow-up album straight away, he spent the next three years practising his stage performance and finishing school.

Then in 1997, Usher's second album, *My Way*, hit the charts and his career really took off. The biggest hit single to come from the album was *You Make Me Wanna*, which was loved by fans and critics alike, especially in the UK. Next came a string of stage appearances as Usher performed with P Diddy, Mary J. Blige and Janet Jackson.

Meanwhile, Usher was becoming a star of the screen too. He appeared in TV shows and films including *She's All That* (1999), with Freddie Prinze Junior, and *Texas Rangers* (2001). He plans to continue building his acting career.

Hit has followed hit, but Usher ran into problems with his third album, *8701*. In 2001, before the album was released, tracks were leaked on the Internet. So Usher went back to the studio and recorded brand new material for the album before it was released. In 2004, *Confessions* sold over one million copies during its first week on sale.

He doesn't always sing alone. In 2004, Usher and fellow R&B singer Alicia Keys reached the top of the US charts with *My Boo*, taken from a special edition of his *Confessions* album. The hit single won a Grammy at the 2005 Awards, while Usher picked up a further two awards for *Confessions* and the single *Yeah!* featuring Lil Jon and Ludacris. But these weren't Usher's first Grammys – he won awards for Best Male R 'n'B Vocal Performance in 2001 and 2002.

Usher's performances are filled with energy and emotion.

"It's scary to think that it's now ten years since the fourteen year old first made his mark on the R&B scene. Yet four albums later, in the wake of multi-platinum sells, he's matured from a teen pop star to a sultry R&B singer of considerable substance."

Lewis Dene – BBC reviewer

weblinks

For more information about Usher, go to
www.waylinks.co.uk/21CentLives/PopStars

Other Pop Stars

Madonna

Her real name is Madonna Louise Ciccone, and she is widely known as the Queen of Pop. Madonna was born on 16 August 1958 in Bay City, Michigan, USA. She always wanted to be a star, studying dance in Michigan before moving to New York. There, she became a professional dancer and sang with punk and pop bands, writing songs in her spare time. In 1983, Madonna had her first hit with *Holiday*, which topped the charts around the world. Since then, she has released over sixty singles and twenty albums in the UK alone, selling more than 250 million records worldwide. Her tours are legendary. On stage she never fails to amaze with extravagant costumes, magnificent sets and crowds of dancers. According to *The Guinness Book of Records*, Madonna is the most successful female recording artist of all time. In 2004 she became one of the first five members of the UK Music Hall of Fame, joining The Beatles, Elvis Presley, Bob Marley and U2.

Joss Stone

Imagine signing a record deal at the age of fourteen… That's exactly what happened to soul singer Joss Stone! She was born Joscelyn Eve Stoker on 11 April 1987 in Dover, England. As she grew up, she discovered that she liked listening to the heartfelt, throaty sound of soul music – and that she liked to sing soul music even more. Her first public performance was at her own comprehensive school. Then, after a live performance on a BBC television junior talent show, Joss was whisked away to New York, where the S-Curve label signed her immediately. Her first album, *The Soul Sessions*, was a compilation of classic soul hits that sold millions of copies. But Joss wanted more from her next venture. She co-wrote most of the tracks from her second album, *Mind, Body and Soul*, which has also been a critical and commercial success. At the 2005 Brit Awards, she won awards for British Female Solo Artist and British Urban Act.

George Michael

He became famous as one half of a 1980s pop duo, but George Michael has been a solo performer for most of his singing career. George was born Georgios Kyriacos Panayiotou in London on 25 June 1963. At school he met Andrew Ridgeley and together they formed the hugely successful pop group, *Wham!* Chart-topping success and brilliant world tours followed, but in 1986 the band decided to split at the very height of their fame. George released his first solo album, *Faith*, the next year and fans were surprised and delighted by his new work. *Faith* became a hit on both sides of the Atlantic and George picked up a stack of awards. More solo albums followed, including *Listen Without Prejudice: Vol. 1, Older, Songs from the Last Century* and *Patience*. Each demonstrated how George's style of songwriting was continually changing and developing. He now rarely performs live, preferring to spend his time writing and recording new material. He is a tireless fundraiser for AIDS charities.

Natasha Bedingfield

Once known only as the younger sister of singer Daniel Bedingfield, Natasha is now a famous pop star in her own right. Born in south-east London on 26 November 1981, Natasha has always loved music. She studied psychology at university, partly because she thought it would help her to understand people and so make her a better songwriter. But it became increasingly difficult to study *and* write songs, so she left college to concentrate on her singing career. Before approaching any record companies, Natasha wrote and recorded her own material. She didn't want to be just another pop star – she wanted to make sure that her music was unique. Her hard work paid off. Natasha's first single, actually called *Single*, reached number three in the UK charts. And her next single did even better, *These Words* reached number one in August 2004. *Unwritten*, her debut album, was released one month later and shot straight to the top of the UK album charts.

Will Young

When Will Young entered the very first UK Pop Idol contest in 2002, he never thought he would win – he just wanted the chance to sing. But Will Young *did* win and found himself at the beginning of a thrilling new career. William Robert Young was born on 20 January 1979 in Berkshire. When he stormed to victory against Gareth Gates in the Pop Idol final, many were surprised. But Will went on to prove to his critics that he *could* be a popstar. In the year after Pop Idol, he scored five UK number one hits, sang in front of the Queen at her Golden Jubilee celebrations, won a Brit Award for Best Newcomer and enjoyed success in Europe. He then took a break to concentrate on songwriting and to develop his own style, which is inspired by soul and jazz music. (Will also gave up smoking to improve his singing – he can now reach higher notes!) His critically acclaimed second album, *Friday's Child*, has sold over a million copies.

Bono

As the lead singer and lyricist of world-famous pop group U2, Paul David Hewson is better known as Bono. He was born in Dublin, Ireland on 10 May 1960. A friend nicknamed him Bono Vox after a type of hearing aid, but this was later shortened to Bono – and the name stuck! In 1976, Bono saw an advert on the school notice board asking if anyone was interested in joining a band. The band eventually became known as U2, releasing their first album in 1980 and their fourteenth in 2004. Bono's voice developed over many years to become the familiar throaty roar of U2's most recent hits. And when smoking threatened to ruin his voice forever, Bono quit at once. Not just a pop star, Bono has another very important career, as an activist who campaigns against global poverty and debt. He is the only singer to feature on both the original 1984 Band Aid single – *Do They Know it's Christmas?* – and the 20th anniversary version by Band Aid 20.

Index